T0128727

SANGIN
Valley

The mental rollercoaster of a Marine
deployed to Sangin, Afghanistan

Mitchell Holmes

authorHOUSE®

AuthorHouse™
1663 Liberty Drive
Bloomington, IN 47403
www.authorhouse.com
Phone: 1 (800) 839-8640

Published by AuthorHouse 04/14/2016

ISBN: 978-1-5246-0362-5 (sc)
ISBN: 978-1-5246-0363-2 (e)

Library of Congress Control Number: 2016906130

Print information available on the last page.

This book is printed on acid-free paper.

Dedications

This book is dedicated to the Marines of 2nd platoon Alpha Company 1st Battalion 5th Marine Regiment who deployed to Sangin, Afghanistan in 2011 and to all the Marines and Sailors who didn't make it home from Sangin.

Acknowledgments

I would like to thank my family and friends who supported me through my years in the Marine Corps and while on deployment. I thank my wife and kids for allowing me to spend countless hours away from them to get this published. I also thank Tim O'Brien, author of The Things They Carried, the book that encouraged me to keep a journal while I was deployed.

Glossary

611: The paved road that runs from the south end to the north end of Sangin, paved by the United States military to provide a safe supplies route to all units in the city

AO: Area of operations
AUP: Afghan Uniformed Police
ANA: Afghan National Army
BC: Battalion Commander
BZO: Battle sight zero
CO: Commanding officer
COG: Corporal of the Guard
DFAC: Dining Facility
DEMIL: Demilitarization, removal of military activity
      or control from an area
EAS: End of active service
EOF: Escalation of force
EOD: Explosive ordinance disposal
FOB: Forward operating Base
HE: High Explosive
HESCO: A modern gabion used for flood control and
      military fortification
IDF: In direct fire
IED: Improvised Explosive Device
KIA: Killed In Action

LP/OP: Listening post Observation post
MRE: Meal ready to eat
NJP: Non judicial punishment
PX: Post Exchange
PB: Patrol Base
POG: Personnel other than grunts
PDHA: Post deployment health assessment
QRF: Quick reaction force
ROE: Rules of engagement
RPG: Rocket propelled grenade
RTB: Return to base
USO: United service organizations
UGR: Unitized group rations
VCP: Vehicle checkpoint
VBIED: Vehicle-borne Improvised Explosive Device

Sangin Valley

March 25, 2011

My name is Mitchell Holmes, I grew up in Cowlitz and Columbia county in Washington and Oregon. I have three sisters and two brothers and both of my parents are living. My childhood dream ever since my second grade Veteran's day assembly has been to join the military, go to combat, then return home, get married and have kids. I remember that assembly like it was yesterday and often think about that day, my Dad took the day off to go to it with me. I even have a picture of us standing on the stage together somewhere and hope I'm able to find it when I get back. That dream has come true, I'm now a Marine with 1st battalion 5th Marine Regiment Alpha company 2nd platoon 2nd squad. Today is the first time in my life that I'm leaving my family and friends to go to a place that I know I may not come back, knowing there's enough of a chance that the Marine Corps even had us write our own obituary and take pictures for the newspaper. It's not easy to leave my family but I'm excited and have wanted to do this since second grade. It's really got me thinking, about life, the past, and the future or if I even have one. Many of the guys seem pretty upset leaving their wives and kids. My biggest fear is what it will do to my family if I don't make it home alive. We said goodbye and waved to our families as the bus drove off. My Mom, Teresa Cahill, Tim Cahill my stepdad, Ross Cahill my little brother and my close friends Bryanna and Steve Kessler were there to watch me leave. My Dad Mike Holmes said goodbye last time I was on leave which was probably easier for both of us than being one more person I feel guilty leaving. When we got on the bus and before it took off Staff Sergeant Praxedus stomped up the steps looking motivated as ever and told us to look outside at our families and said we have to fight every fucking day to get back to them. We left March Air force base to Bangor, Maine, then to Leipzig, Germany. After a couple hours there we flew to Manas, Kyrgyzstan. At Manas I learned that the Airforce calls what we call a chow hall, a DFAC and they are much nicer than our chow halls. Here is where it was put in perspective how much different we are from the other branches, but damn, their cooks cook real food instead of just adding water to the powdered eggs and heating stuff up in the oven.

Mitchell and Michael Holmes at Mitchell's 2nd grade Veterans Day assembly.

Sangin Valley

March 29, 2011

Today we arrived at Camp Leatherneck in Afghanistan. We will stay here for a few days to acclimatize, prepare ourselves for what the next seven months brings, and whatever else the higher ups have to do before we fly into Sangin. It's a lot bigger camp than I've always pictured. It reminds me of twenty-nine palms, California in ways, not a wonderful place to be reminded of but that's what it has me thinking about. Most of the vehicles here are Mercedes-Benz and Toyotas driven by foreign contractors. Transportation around the camp is by bus, there's a color coded route system that we have yet to figure out what color bus goes where and at what times. But we really don't need to figure it out since we don't intend to be here very long. The DFACs here are pretty good, we wish we could take one with us, we already know Sangin won't have one. It sounds like MREs, UGRs, and whatever we get in care packages for seven months. It's pretty boring here and the USO has long waiting lines for the phones and computers, it hasn't been long enough without them to want to wait that long. Plus we are all anxious to do what we been training the last year to do and came here for.

March 30, 2011

Went to the Barma lanes, went through some IED lanes and sat through a briefing on the materials and types of IEDs being used in our soon to be area of operations. Then got to look at it all closely so we have an idea what we're looking for and things to be cautious

3

of when we get out there on patrol. Also went to the BZO range to confirm our rifles are accurate at both day and night and to double check that all our optics are working properly.

March 31, 2011

Today we went to an ROE brief to learn the rules of engagement for the area at this time. Until today I never fully understood how many rules there was to war. I've always heard about the Geneva Convention but didn't know what all it consisted of. And in this case we are the only ones that are following them. The Taliban won't hesitate to cut our head off with a dull knife and take pictures with it right before they parade it up and down the streets but we have to treat them like humans if we detain them for committing a terrorist attack or trying to kill us. Staff Sergeant Praxedus sat the platoon down afterwards and asked us how we are feeling about everything and asked if anyone had any questions that he could answer, he does this occasionally to check the morale of the platoon and answer any questions he has an answer to.

April 2, 2011

The jokes that have been thrown around the last year about going home with no legs have pretty much stopped, reality has set in and we all know it's possible that it will happen to a few of us, it's not funny to anyone anymore. Lance Corporal William Baltes and I talked today about our childhoods, how we were raised, how we used to build forts, make fake guns, roll up grass in pieces of newspaper and try to smoke it then sit all day to get a shot at the invisible enemy, and how we used to play with GI Joes as a kid. We have a more similar past and more in common than we ever realized just bullshitting in training and hanging out on the weekends, etc. No one seems to hate it here or hate each other yet, everyone is still getting along pretty good.

April 4, 2011

Today we flew in to FOB Nolay at the southern end of Sangin. Here is where this dream turned into a reality really fast as they dispersed ammo and explained immediate action for the convoy that would be taking us to our destination patrol bases. We then took trucks to PB Uzman, dropped off everyone who was going there, then came to PB Gumbatty where we will stand post and operate out of for a while. Today I stood my first six hour post with a Marine from the unit that's been here the past seven months so he can bring me up to speed on the people, the activity in the area, how they have been doing things and anything else that they can teach us to help us be safe and successful. This transition period is called the rip. I experienced a sort of culture shock that I have never came close to experiencing before as the sun came up and the locals started their day. Seeing how these people live, their poor hygiene, their shitty living conditions, and their over populated compounds, having to work all day every day just to survive and how far in technology this city is behind us, makes me wish Americans could see this, it would make people more appreciative for what they do have.

April 5, 2011

Today we took a detainee who was found to be a bomb maker after investigating his suspicious behavior. When he was first spotted he was on top of a roof and kept ducking down acting like he didn't want any of us to see him so the AUP went and drug him out of the house into the street then brought him in. They made him cry on their way up the road, dragging him and beating the shit out of him the whole way. They seem so far to be pretty easy to get along with. Even though I have no fucking clue most of what they are saying, they talk fast and talk a lot even after I tell them I don't understand what they are saying over and over again. They don't know most of what I'm saying either but we have conversations by what we do know of each other's language and by playing charades. They are kind of weird conversations, with lots of guessing involved. One of them is supposed to stand post with us at all times to be learning from us to be able to protect their own country, even though they don't pay much attention and they fall asleep a lot, they are there with us if we need them or need something checked out outside our walls. Some of them are very willing to learn. One of them named Mama is determined to go to Lashkar Gah and learn English, then move to America, he keeps telling me that while showing me he wants to go on an airplane. They are constantly watching porn and saying jiggy jiggy to us then laughing like little kids. Jiggy jiggy means sex in Pashtu. The AUP Commander wakes up his guys by yelling, slapping and dumping water on them. That normally gets them moving pretty quickly. They will go to the bizarre for us if we ask them to, give them money, and let them know in some way what we want. They have welcomed us here already and have been bringing us food, some of which is better than some of our food back home. I don't know why we're eating it or what's in most of it but it's pretty good so we are. I'm sure we will pay for it later, that's probably why they gave us so many shots before we deployed. The way everything looks around here makes me wonder why we're even touching any of it…but we are.

April 6, 2011

Today a local national stopped by Gumbatty and talked to the Marine on post one about filing a claim for a wall that one of our patrols had destroyed recently. It's a counter insurgency effort to pay for things we damage, hire the locals to do things they are capable of doing that we don't have the equipment for, time, manpower etc., in hope that they will become friends with us, become loyal to us, support us, and help us instead of helping the enemy with their cowardly ways of fighting. The days are going by slow and I'm standing a lot of post. Damn plate carrier got heavy fast. We are expecting things to heat up and get hectic with the summer approaching and the poppy about ready to be harvested. Harvest time means the Taliban have to be close by, waiting to take their cut as soon as all these farmers harvest. Thankfully we haven't had any casualties so far. We are dreading that it could happen at any time to any one of us.

April 9, 2011

We finally received contact at the picket, around midnight last night. It was small arms fire and we returned shots. The AUP took shots from post two at Gumbatty but we're doubting they saw anything, they randomly shoot at birds, carry their rifles in a bunch of different unusual ways, they never know if it's loaded or not and are just all together unorganized and uncoordinated. It was a stormy night they decided to hit us, the blimp was down, it was raining, windy, thunder, and lightening, us at a disadvantage due to lessened visibility and still not completely familiar with the area. I got mail today from my Mom, and hugs from home, an organization that donates and sends care packages to troops that are deployed. I'm looking forward to getting enough manpower here to be able to run patrols further than just to the picket and back and see more of the area. I've been thinking a lot about what my old friends are doing with their life, some are in school, some are raising kids, some got into good jobs straight out of high school. I'm not having 2nd thoughts but I am trying hard to reassure myself that I made the right decision and that what I'm doing really means something to myself, my family and our country. I'm definitely excited to go home knowing that I'll have done more at twenty years old than many people do in an entire lifetime. I'm starting to look at life with a different perspective, and really getting to see how easy and good Americans have it compared to the people of Afghanistan or the people of any third world country. It makes me want to live a better life and do more when I return home.

April 14, 2011

I haven't been able to make any time to write for the last few days, though I wish I was able to write more, I've been pretty busy. 1st squad is now at Gumbatty with us. Standing Post is still long because we are running patrols everyday too. I share a room with Lance Corporal Joseph Lechnar, Lance Corporal Ulysses Lopez, Lance Corporal William Baltes, and Lance Corporal Corey Gibbs. It's about big enough for three people in here but we got five of us in here with all of our gear, it seems as if the room is shrinking. We have one doorway with no door that we're going to have to find something to act as a door, no windows, carpet and a light that will sometimes turn on if we flip the switch (two bare wires that you touch together), the power here doesn't work like it does back home. I was informed a few days ago that Corporal Tony Mullis, one of the engineers attached to 1/5 that we trained with at twenty-nine palms, hit an IED and lost both legs, luckily he lived and will be okay. He's been the only casualty at this time but they are expecting things to get a lot worse, we been training for it for over a year and we are as ready as we're ever going to be. We got a new batch of AUP and I don't really like them, no one really does, these guys were brought in from the bigger cities to work here for a set period of time, then leave to go somewhere else, therefore they aren't fighting for their hometown so their attitude is different, they don't want to get killed for a paycheck. The other guys were from Sangin so they were motivated to try to protect it, being their home. I miss them already even though I just met them less than two weeks ago. I'm starting to miss home a little bit but glad I'm here chasing my dream, maybe part of it is just knowing we got a long time before we get to go home, makes it a little overwhelming. It's too early for this and I shouldn't even be thinking about going home yet. When we do go home I intend to not take things for granted like I used to, it's the simple things in life that no one ever stops to think about what it would be like without them. Running water, hot water, lights with a light switch, grocery stores, cell phones, I could go on and on but not going to. I have a feeling it will be kind of a culture shock again going back home after spending seven months here and I'm hoping things will seem easier than they were before. I think this may be one of the hardest things a man can endure. It's probably even harder for the guys who are married and/or have kids at home counting on them to come home to them. I can only imagine how hard this experience must be on them and their families.

Ulysses Lopez and Mitchell Holmes
at Mojave Viper training.

April 15, 2011

We went on our First patrol in the brown zone today. The brown zone is made up of compounds, roads, very little vegetation, hills, and alley ways, some known to be full of IEDs that we don't dare go down. It was quite an experience going down alleys and over ground where Marines have been killed that we been hearing about the last year, it makes my mind think faster than I can process it all. We blew up a wall and firing position while out on patrol. Also stopped by PB Uzman and visited 3rd squad. Patrolled through the cemetery on the way back, it smelt like fucking shit, and looked about the same. It must have had some fresh bodies rotting in the heat. Their funerals are a lot different than ours back in America, they dig a shallow grave, then put the body in it wrapped in some kind of cloth, then pile rocks on top of them. Then decorate it and do whatever religious and traditional things they do. We're patrolling again tomorrow, It's not bad other carrying the THOR. It's not that it's that heavy but the son of a bitch is awkward as fuck and cuts off circulation to both arms and I haven't figured out a way yet to wear it without the straps digging in. Whoever designed it didn't design it to fit over a camelback and clearly had never worn one around while wearing a plate carrier, one or the other is doable without bitching about it too much but not while trying to carry both.

The brown zone in Sangin, Afghanistan.

April 16, 2011

We patrolled the brown zone again today. First thing, we went up Pharmacy road, the most dangerous road in Sangin at one point before we got here, loaded with IEDs and the area surrounding full of murder holes. Murder holes are holes in walls used by the Taliban to surprise us and shoot from, with the ability to get away without us seeing where they went or being able to pursue them. Usually in choke points that don't allow us to go anywhere but forward or back. We been getting mail every couple days and no one is bitching about that. It's a morale booster getting mail and it always brightens our day. We are all missing home, probably even more than we will admit to each other but we are all doing fine. Everyone is saying they won't take things for granted when we get back home after living in these conditions for seven months. Everyone seems to be handling it all in their own way. I'm seeing more of my buddies now that 1st squad is here at Gumbatty with us. Most of The kids have started to become irritating and frustrate us, always getting really close, grabbing at our gear, reaching in our drop pouch and asking for chocolate. And it's hard when they don't listen when we say no because there's not a whole lot else we can do without putting hands on them. A lot of the guys have been getting sick as fuck, puking their guts out, even though we got lots of shots, something is still getting to them. I'm hoping I get lucky and don't catch anything with as much shit as I've been giving the rest of 2nd squad for being pussies and missing patrols to lay around playing sick.

April 18, 2011

We patrolled for the first time in the green zone today. The green zone is an area with fewer compounds than the brown zone, canals used for irrigation, fields for crops, and the majority of the poppy and green vegetation in the valley. It runs parallel with the Helmand River. Today I carried the ladder, we used it a few times to provide over watch and to cross canals, not only to keep from getting wet but also to avoid triggering any water borne IEDs. Lieutenant Viehmeyer, Baltes, and Mongal our interpreter still managed to fall in though. Lieutenant Colonel Savage, 1st Battalion 5th Marines battalion commander patrolled with us and afterwards said he was pleased with the patrol and the conduct and professionalism of our squad. It was a successful day with no casualties and we learned a lot about the area we will be operating in for the following months. Lopez got NJP for not having his gloves on while on post. We also aren't supposed to wear white socks because it's against regulation. Even though we strongly believe that it's more important to be able to walk, run, and preform our daily duties than for all of us to look cute and match. I'm continuing to have white socks sent from home, those of us who want to wear white socks cut the tops off some brown ones and slip them over the tops so if some miserable asshole comes around checking sock color, it looks as if we are all wearing brown socks. I guess IEDs must discriminate against what color socks we are wearing...They told us today that after patrols our grenades and 40mm rounds have to be turned in and locked up instead of having it in our room easily accessible. I sure hope we don't need any during the night when it's all locked up. I finally took the time and showered yesterday for the first time in three weeks in a makeshift shower that Corporal Lindley built with hesco and a collapsible water jug that would normally be used for camping. Staff Sergeant had the AUP pick up some food from the bizarre so we ate pretty well the last couple nights and Sergeant Byrd did the cooking. MREs and UGRs got old really fast, same shit day after day and the UGRs never seem to get cooked all the way through, it's kind of like getting hard eggs at the chow hall and knowing it's hard because the powdered eggs didn't get mixed all the way. Well I've probably bitched enough for the day, if anyone ever reads this they're probably going think I'm a whiny motherfucker by now and not even want to finish reading the whole thing.

April 20, 2011

Well today I'm back on the picket with Baltes and Lance Corporal McAfee. First time I've got to hang out with McAfee since we been here. Got off the picket yesterday morning, went on post, got off post six hours later, unloaded pallets of bottled water, and then went to sleep. Woke up, fixed some drainage, then moved the burn pit out to the other end of the PB away from where everyone sleeps so maybe we can avoid getting sick from that on top of everything else. The engineers came in and enlarged our PB so 3rd squad can move in and the whole platoon be together again, once they got done we filled and moved sandbags to fill the holes in the wall, then fixed the c wire. Now back on the picket for twenty four hours. We haven't got mail for a few days so hopefully we will tonight. We're overdue and everyone needs restocked. Only a month down and we're all ready to go home. Everyone's reasons for being here are different but we will all take some positive things away from it too. It's an experience I wish everyone could have the opportunity to experience. It gives you a different perspective on life and makes you happy with what you have instead of always thinking about what you don't have and think you need. Americans take things for granted, myself included and kids in America are so much different than the ones here. These people have so little to show for their life and have grown up and live their lives every day in a war torn environment full of hatred and violence, yet are so happy about the smallest things. They make do with what they have or what they can work for. The kids spend their days walking around shooting stuff with sling shots, throwing rocks at each other, and hassling Marines. How many American kids would rather go play outside with sling shots and whatever they could find outside to make a game out of than sit inside on a sunny day playing videogames and watching TV.

Mitchell Holmes and friendly local kid on a bicycle.

April 22, 2011

For the most part everything is still mostly quiet and boring. The Malaria pills we have to take are giving us crazy dreams and makes it hard to want to sleep wondering what our mind will do to us. Corporal Prince and Corporal Geboo are now with 1st and 2nd squad so they are here at Gumbatty with us.

April 23, 2011

We patrolled the green zone today. Part of the route we took we had never traveled before, it was a rough trail but was a good patrol overall and educational. We work the opposite of water, we take the path of most resistance. That way it reduces our chance of walking on an IED, they mainly place them on heavily traveled areas or where they think we will take cover when they take pop shots at us. They try to use our training to their advantage. We talked to some kids today that said the Taliban left and aren't coming back but we doubt it considering they don't just leave that easily and are suspicious as to why those kids would even tell us that if they considered that we may suspect them helping the enemy. I been thinking a lot about all the things I have and always have had that I didn't pay enough attention to until I came here. Also about all the things I've done wrong. I'm becoming closer to people that I would have never expected to and farther apart from people I always thought I'd be close to no matter what. I wouldn't say I'm having a blast but it is fun here at times and we find ways to make each other laugh and pass the time. I know deep down my reasons for being here and that it's my dream and always has been, that will continue to push me to keep moving every day and never give up.

April 24, 2011

Today is Easter day, a happy day for most people but a sad day for Alpha Company. Lance Corporal Joe M. Jackson from 3rd platoon was killed today by an IED. Joe was the company's first KIA. It has greatly affected everyone but we have a job to do and have to keep pushing. That's what Joe would expect from all of us. Hopefully the feelings this has created keeps everyone from being complacent and from allowing any casualties to happen if we can prevent it. I can't quit thinking about what Joe's family is going through and how his death will change their lives forever. We went on a five hour patrol to Uzman to drop off Lieutenant Veihmeyer, then patrolled into the green zone, to star wars(a nickname for an area in the green zone), and could see the Helmand River. We could see the mysterious unexplored land across the river too, it kind of gave me goosebumps at the thought of what could be over there. Came out in 2/8 AO and the people were mean mugging the shit out of us, there had to have been something up with them. They were a lot different than the people near Gumbatty. They have no problem making it obvious if they like us or hate us. Some of the people will even lead us through the areas around their homes that they know are clear and show us where any IEDs are that they are aware of. It's hard knowing which ones are trustworthy though. Not sure if it's because they are being nice and want to help us or because they don't want us stomping on their crops. Their crops are their lifeline, and after the Taliban taxes them and takes their cut to fund their terrorist activities, it only leaves the people with limited resources and money to survive off and take care of their families.

April 25, 2011

We got some mail today. I got six packages from my Mom, Tim, and Ross, one from the Cook family, and one from my sister Cori. Got off the picket, getting ready to go on post for eighteen hours so 1st squad can do a long cordon and knock operation tomorrow. Step off time is 0400. I'm not really excited for this eighteen hour post but it has to be done and only makes us that much stronger...and tired. It's probably way too early to even be talking about it but we've already been talking about the things we're going to do when we get home. 1/5 is going to tear Vegas up while we're there for the Marine Corps Ball in November. I've been becoming closer to Baltes, the more we talk the more we find we have in common and we are able to keep a conversation going for about as long as we can stay awake. Thinking a lot about what I want to do with my life in the future too when I'm done with this. Get married? Have Kids? Re-enlist? Make the Marine Corps a career? Keep deploying? Go back to school? Get out? Fuck there's too much time to think. I've always wanted a family as soon as I returned home from a deployment but I don't think I can balance this lifestyle with a family. I don't feel like it would be fair to them to be gone all the time and leave for deployments leaving them to wonder if you are coming home or not. I already feel bad for what I've put my family through coming here. I don't know if I could do it to them again. A lot going through my mind right now.

April 26, 2011

Got off post at twelve, called my Mom to check in and let her know everything is going alright. At least to give her a couple minutes of relief while we're on the phone, I'm sure it's the only time she's not worried. I'm Glad to hear from her that there's so many people that support us and are thinking about us back home. There's a lot of people to thank and visit when I get back. We got word about a Kandahar prison escape with an estimated five hundred insurgents here in Afghanistan. It was a warm day today at the picket with Lechnar and Lance Corporal Ledbetter. Being out here with guys that are easy to get along with sure makes the time pass by a lot faster and smoother.

April 28, 2011

1st platoon took a casualty today, one of their combat engineers. That's our company's 5th. Baltes and I been getting fucked over the last four days. Got off post at 1800 and were told we were going to the picket. It's nice of them to fuck us constantly when we know for a fact there's some pricks who are getting hooked up and been off for over twenty four hours bragging about how much time they've had off and that they are running out of things to do in their spare time. They aren't much of team players but haven't been since we met so I don't know why I expected anything to change. Maybe I just bitch too much but I can't begin to understand why they get to sleep and play games while we do everything and don't even bitch about it out loud. On paper and to each other amongst our squad is the only bitching we do. The rumor now is that were getting relieved and pushing to the mountains or Kajaki which is seventeen miles north of where we are now but who knows, the Lance Corporal underground spreads a lot of shit, a lot of which turns out to be true but not all of it, so we will just have to wait and see what happens.

April 30, 2011

We set up and Stayed at an LP/OP last night in the brown zone. I wasn't on the first shift of post and Mongal brought us all chai from the owner of the compound. We sat in a circle, drank chai and bullshitted with Mongal until Sergeant Elizondo told us to shut the fuck up and go to sleep. Mongal often talks about America and is excited to move there. He's pretty educated on American culture and what it's like in the states. I think everyone back home would like him and think he's pretty funny. As much time as he's spent living with Marines over the last few years I'd say he's pretty much corrupted and has become a lot like us. We are now pushing two patrols a day even though we don't want to or really have the desired manpower to run two a day and maintain the PB. Everyone is worn out and becoming more complacent and careless as the days go by. Not about each other, or our families, but about ourselves. It's a hard feeling to explain. At times I worry about some of the guys doing something crazy or hurting themselves. Everyone seems a little down and depressed, maybe because we haven't got mail for a few days and that's what gives us motivation, and hope that there will be an end. CAT came and took over the picket yesterday so we thought that would give us a couple extra guys to throw into the rotation to make things a little easier on everyone but the increase in patrols makes it so our workload remains the same so no one is really happy.

May 2, 2011

Did Lots of post standing today. 1st squad took the Company Commander and 1st Sergeant with them on patrol today and they were hit by a suicide bomber wearing an explosive vest that walked into the middle of their patrol and blew himself up killing one of the AUP and Corporal Lindley took a ball bearing to his collar bone and was taken to bastion. The offensive was supposed to start yesterday and it very well did. None of the squads patrolled yesterday. The whole platoon worked on reinforcing the PB to prepare for possible attacks and took a detainee. A guy who has been tailing patrols, walking back and forth past our PB trying to look inside every time he gets a chance, whistling at night when a convoy was approaching, and trying to sell us hashish out at the picket. When the AUP commander asked him about the hashish he denied it, then when he searched him and found some in his pocket he slapped that guy harder I think than I've ever seen someone slapped. The guy dropped down to his knees and was instantly crying and apologizing for lying about it.

Tanner Lindley and Mitchell Holmes

May 3, 2011

We patrolled down into 2/8 AO this morning but had to RTB because 2/8 wasn't notified that we would be crossing into their AO. It was a short patrol but a good one, the THOR is getting heavier by the day but we have to have three of them on each patrol to cover all possibilities. We're taking a different approach with the locals after yesterday's bombing, making them stop a long distance away from us and lift their shirt to see if they got a suicide vest on and making them go around the patrol instead of letting them walk right through the middle of it. The mobile PX came tonight, I was able to stock up on cigarettes since our mail hasn't been making it to us for some reason. We've heard it's in the vicinity but not making it to our PB. They know mail is our motivation, hopefully Staff Sergeant can get it moving. He's good about being persistent and not stopping till he gets what he wants. We all respect him when it comes to that, he will go out of his way and do anything for us. We were told today that Osama Bin Laden was killed but we know that won't change anything here other than that the AUP are driving around like idiots screaming and telling us about it over and over again like it's a new holiday.

May 4, 2011

Our squad set up a snap VCP this morning in the cemetery hoping to get someone to try to pull a fast one on us. Nothing out of the ordinary though. A short patrol, got back and went on post an hour later. A sand storm then hit us followed by rain, thunder, and lightning while we were on post. Then got off post to find out we go back on at midnight. We can't wait till Corporal Lindley gets back from Camp leatherneck, he's the only one that stands up for us and will speak his mind no matter what the consequences may be. They tried sending him home but he's causing all sorts of hell writing letters up the chain of command saying he wants to get back to his Marines, not go home. His methods and attitude towards everything is different from the others, but he is a true leader that we all respect and look up to. He looks out for his Marines and their welfare. And that's his first priority, he doesn't care about rank and medals, or what u think of him, he cares about us before anything.

May 5, 2011

I feel like I'm losing my mind today, I think sleep deprivation is starting to set in. I had a good thoughtful conversation with Baltes today for nine hours on post together though. We talked a lot about the past, present, and the future, things we would go back and do different if we could, things we need to do different now and in our future. The whole squad is starting to become really close. We spent a lot of time together stateside and through the workup, but being deployed together has made us a million times closer. Even with the shitty day to day conditions we manage to laugh and have a good time by making Nicknames for each other, pranking each other, playing monopoly, etc. It keeps us busy when we're not on post or patrolling. Hopefully I'll get some sleep tonight and get to play catch up a little bit. Because of the AUP that was killed by the suicide bomber the AUP had a feast and fed us as much as we could eat, they invited police from other PBs, and threw what seemed like a party, kind of like what we would do as a celebration of life. They seem like decent people and seem to care a lot about us too. They are always giving us stuff and eager to learn from us. Hopefully in time we will be able to teach them to defend their own ground so we don't have to lose American lives anymore for their cause. They gained my respect when one of them was killed going to search the suicide bomber. That tells me that at least some of them are willing to fight and die for the cause, and if we're here willing to then they definitely should too.

May 6, 2011

3rd squad moved in to Gumbatty today, 1st squad moved over to Uzman. We started to do a two week rotation to Uzman to give everyone a two week break from patrolling. It's just standing six hour posts with no patrols and very few working party's. We will leave for Uzman in two weeks for our first break. It's good to see the guys from 3rd squad for a couple weeks, we haven't seen much of them in six weeks we've been here. I went to the picket today and helped build a tower to replace the vehicles. We had to hand fill hesco that was too high for the engineer's equipment to reach and dump into. It was either that or have the tower be shorter and more vulnerable. It was a pretty simple day and kind of a break compared to the way things been going lately.

May 7, 2011

We went today and checked out the clinic by the bizarre, mission changed as soon as we left, it was a short distanced patrol but had long security halts. We are slowly becoming closer with the AUP trying to build a working relationship and some sort of trust in each other. Their cook always brings rice to our room even when we don't want any so we're trying to find a way or something to give him to show our appreciation and return the kind gesture. I'm having a hard time figuring out what they would like or use though.

May 8, 2011

Today brought more post with Baltes. We talked a lot about next year's workup and what things will be like when our leadership leaves and we become the new leadership of 2nd platoon. We named one of the AUP that was on post with us. He's a real little guy, pretty quiet, and friendly. We decided to nickname him Pee

Wee and he laughed and said good so that's what we're calling him from now on. When we got off post we built a garbage can, a big shelf and some little shelves for our room. We had fun doing it even if the rest of the guys did laugh at us for it. It made us feel more at home doing projects. Or maybe it has to do with finally getting a little break and being able to do something. Now we're setting everything that will fit on our shelves on them trying to piss off the rest of our room by asking them how jealous they are and how long it's going to be before they ask us to build them one. The company is doing a hard knock operation tomorrow, our platoon and 1st platoon to go raid a compound that we have Intel saying it's got terrorist activity associated with it. Gibbs and I been talking a lot, have become friends and becoming closer by the day. We hated each other when we first met and I'm really not even sure why and for a long time after. Just got off to a bad start I guess. I never would have thought we would become friends and as close as we are now but we have. As much writing as I do, I shouldn't be bitching about not sleeping enough. So I guess I better get to bed, we got a long day ahead of us tomorrow.

Corey Gibbs and Mitchell Holmes at PB Uzman.

May 9, 2011

I didn't go on the operation today, I was one of the five that stayed back and stood post the whole time. It turned out to be a harmless schoolhouse anyway so those of us who stayed back didn't miss anything exciting. The few of us that stayed back stood nine hours of post then attempted to sleep, failed at the attempt to sleep, then went and set up a snap VCP by the bridge by post two. This time stuck with one of the girls that's with the FET team who doesn't speak a word of Pashtu that asked me to translate or to get the interpreter so she could talk to the women. The Female Engagement Team, to me that would require learning how to speak Pashtu fairly fluently so they could talk to the women because they are more likely to talk to them being women than us being men. But that defeats their purpose if they have to go through a man to be able to communicate. Holy fucking shit, I would think they would learn at least the basics to be able to attempt talking to the women. I think the FET could be very helpful if it operated differently. Post again at midnight, but at least it's with Gibbs so we can bullshit all night. Everyone is really hating this place about now, especially the ones who stand a lot of post, staring at the same thing day after day gets old. Corporal Lindley came back to Gumbatty today, I haven't had a chance to talk to him yet but looking forward to it and there's a few of us who are sure glad he's back.

May 10, 2011

Stood post with Gibbs this morning. We talked the whole time about all kids of random shit and told random stories that no one has ever been interested in before and that I think both of us just thought we needed to tell someone, it was interesting and made six hours fly by in no time. Slept when we got off, then patrolled to the clinic to talk with the doctor and run people through the system. One guy popped, he was caught with weapons a few years back and got away so we turned him into FOB Nolay to process him and they decide what to do with him from there on out. Apache mobile is supposed to be on their way from Nolay with a bunch of mail so we're waiting impatiently thinking about what's in there waiting for us and who we're going to hear from back home. Pine lights are getting old and my dad has been sending Marlboro 27s every two weeks so I'm hoping there's some in there today.

May 11, 2011

We patrolled to the schoolhouse today and apologized for the raid the other day and explained to them why it happened without giving them too much information in case they are hiding weapons or helping the Taliban in some way and are just really good at hiding it. It seemed to go really well though and seems that we have their support in the efforts to drive the Taliban out. Were possibly going to the green zone tomorrow in search of a high value target.

May 12, 2011

It's been a pretty boring day here. I Stood eight hours post, then went and wrote a few letters home and tried sleeping but it's hard when it feels like you're lying in an oven even when you are out of the sun and its midnight. Once I accepted that I wouldn't be able to sleep I went and bullshitted with the guys and sat around the rest of the day. The satellite phone is broke so all we can do is write home and wait for a response, but I'm ok with that, I don't call home a lot, not that I don't want to its just hard knowing what to say and I'm not good at the whole emotional thing, I don't like hearing people sad or crying.

May 13, 2011

We patrolled the brown zone today and took HET to talk to the teacher at the schoolhouse and put more people in the system, got mail from people I don't know but they are friends of my sister Cori. It's always nice to know we have support from people we do and don't know.

Today I Stood post with Lance Corporal Waupoose, a 0331 machine gunner that's under Corporal Lindley's command. They are both from weapons platoon but are attached to our platoon for the deployment. It's good to talk to someone different for a change that I don't really know that well, so we're not always talking about the same shit over and over again with the same assholes we always talk to.

May 14, 2011

I stood post this morning then had some off time. Talked a lot with the guys in the squad today. Everyone's thoughts and feelings about deployment and life are constantly changing. It seems like life gets more and more confusing every day, maybe overthinking everything. I keep wondering if we will look back on how we feel now, in five months, a year, or ten years and if it will feel the same or if we will even remember what it felt like or be able to make any sense out of it. I often wonder how much my Dad remembers from Vietnam and how much he just doesn't talk about or has tried to forget. And wonder how hard it will be to adjust to normal life when we go home. If our family and friends will be different or if they will think we are significantly different. I hope this doesn't completely change me. I think we all are feeling some depth of depression and missing home, especially the married guys or the guys that have kids. Everyone is at each other's throat 24/7, it's a big pissing match between the squads. I keep waiting for some fights to break out. Baltes, Gibbs and I get along great, and get along ok with most of our squad but not so much with everyone else. We just try to keep to ourselves and count on each other but not to expect much from most of the guys from the other squads. We were told deployment would bring us all close together, for a few of us that's very much true but with the others I think it's made us grow farther apart, even grown apart from the guys we always spent the weekends drinking and partying with the whole workup.

May 15, 2011

We did a security patrol around Gumbatty today. We found a firing position that needs blown, met some of the locals, and learned the area right directly around our PB, some of which we didn't realize exactly what was there until today. The tall walls make it hard to see very far and allow the enemy to move freely closely around us. I think today may have been the hottest day since we been here. I started working out with Baltes today. I'm hoping to go home bigger than I came here instead of going home smaller like most of the guys are going to. I don't really have much weight to lose so I should and hopefully will put on some weight. We're supposed to be doing our rotation to Uzman on Saturday, we're all ready for a break from Gumbatty and all of its bullshit and drama. It sounds like there's more action over there anyway. There's still a lot weighing on my mind. Lots of Confusion and Frustration about myself.

May 16, 2011

It was hot as fuck on the picket today stuck in vehicles with no A/C. I did though successfully cook top ramen in a brown MRE bag sitting in the sun for about ten minutes, that's how hot it was. We're hating all the kids except for one right now named Putagay. He's very respectful and wants to be friends with us. He's the only kid that doesn't ask for anything, doesn't throw rocks at us nonstop and that tries to hold a conversation about one subject without taking off and talking to someone else. He seems very mature for eight years old and even tells the other kids to back up or leave us alone. In return for not begging for stuff or irritating us, I always carry something and hold on to it to give him when I see him.

Putagay, Mitchell's local friend, also
liked by everyone in 2nd squad.

May 17, 2011

Went on post from midnight to 0600, then went straight on a patrol to the green zone. Abdul one of the AUP really pissed me off today, he got mad when I wouldn't let him sit down on patrol and drag his rifle in the dirt behind him, and I could tell he was stoned out of his mind like always, he's a real piece of shit and I wish he would be relieved, I don't trust him being on patrol with us. We took pop shots then had to RTB because 2/8 denied us access to pursue. Waiting to go on post at midnight. Wondering if the whole deployment is going to be like this. But on a positive note, a couple of us who want to workout started to build a gym tonight, so when it's done we can go there to take out our anger. It feels good to start working out again after so long not doing it.

May 18, 2011

I went on Post from midnight to six. Then filled sandbags to reinforce the north wall, then went back on post at twelve. Got off at 2000, had a squad talk about the way things have been going with the platoon, then I geared up and went and talked to Lechnar on post. When I left Lechnar's post I went and talked to McAfee since I don't see him much anymore. I don't see much of anyone outside 2nd squad with the busy schedule that we are on.

May 19, 2011

The tower at the picket was finished today so now we won't have to bake in the vehicles out there with no air conditioning anymore for twenty four hours at a time. The tower has a big post on top and a room below it that allows the guys resting to take their gear off and actually rest. That will make things a little bit easier for everyone. We're going to Uzman tomorrow, definitely beyond ready to go but it sucks we have to leave Lechnar behind since he's the brains of the platoon and has been to a few schools to learn stuff the rest of us don't know.

May 20, 2011

2nd squad is At Uzman now for two weeks. Hopefully we will get some rest and time to work out. I've got a ton of mail I haven't got around to opening yet, but every time we get mail I sure do feel like a lot of people care. Pretty excited to be here with just our squad. There's only three posts here with eight of us so sometimes we will get twelve hours off.

May 21, 2011

I got off post and did some organizing in our room. Sergeant Elizondo cooked the stuff I got from Shannon one of the AUP here at Uzman. Everyone was happy to eat something different for a change. I got the opportunity to get a video this morning of a goat being killed and butchered, first time I've watched someone cut a goat's throat from the standing position to kill it then burn all the hair off with a torch. Probably a once in a lifetime experience. Sergeant Delagarza and another guy from 3rd platoon got hit today by an IED, grenade, and then small arms fire. I heard it all as it was happening come across the radio. I go on post in a few hours, going to go workout and maybe write a few letters first though I suppose. Things have been heating up lately, maybe tonight will bring some excitement.

Moises Espinal, Juan Elizondo,
Mitchell Holmes, and Agustin Amador at
Bridgeport mountain warfare training.

May 23, 2011

Got off post, worked out for a while, went to sleep, then woke up and Gibbs and I cooked a combination of random stuff from care packages mixed with potatoes I got the AUP to pick up from the bizarre with his new hotplate that his Dad sent him. Now we're just waiting to go on post, there's so much time here I don't know what to do with it but I'm not complaining, I can keep myself busy. Sure a big change being here from Gumbatty. There's lots of time to think, too much time to think. Thinking too much will drive a guy crazy.

May 24, 2011

There's sure not a lot that goes on here at Uzman. There's post, then eat, then sleep, then workout, then do it all over again, but the break is sure nice. The ANA stepped on an IED nearby today. We been hearing that we are getting rid of Uzman in a couple weeks, but also hearing we may start running fire team size patrols out of here with a squad of ANP, I sure hope I'm not a part of that fire team…we Got mail today. I think getting mail here is almost exciting as when I used to get the letters from my oldest sister Carla in the mail even though she only lived a few miles away, a childhood memory I'll never forget. I can remember it so clearly, it seems like just yesterday.

May 25, 2011

The mobile PX came today, Gibbs and I both stocked up on protein and dip, then went and worked out. Now I'm just writing, listening to music, eating, and waiting to go on post later. It's not super exciting but I'm definitely not going to complain, it gives us plenty of time to rest and workout. I'm kind of starting to wish I had a lot more music on this iPod though, I'm going to know all these songs by heart by the time we go home.

May 26, 2011

Slept a lot today and worked out when I got up. 3rd squad found three freshly planted IEDs somewhere in the brown zone. They stopped by afterwards and said Gumbatty has gotten worse since we left, then got pissed when we said no shit because we're here and they are there changing everything around, changing the way we've been doing things the whole time just to make it easier on them. We're not really excited to have to go back there.

May 29, 2011

I been working out a lot lately. Becoming close friends with Gibbs. We have a lot in common, a lot of the same morals, we share the same interests, have a lot of similar goals in life, and we were brought up the same way. The CO stopped by today and confirmed that Uzman is being turned over to the ANA but not sure exactly when. Still waiting to get mail from a couple certain people. Finally got a new M203 for my rifle that works.

June 4, 2011

I haven't wrote for a few days because I'm back to Gumbatty and haven't had the time to do much of anything other than post and moving back over here. We got back here yesterday and it surprisingly seems to be better than when we were here last. There's less working parties, some improvements to make things easier on us, etc. I'm at the new picket tower with Baltes. I've known Gibbs for the shortest amount of time of anyone in the platoon but he has become my closest friend. We visit each other on post just to bullshit and pass time because we understand each other and I don't get irritated with him, and I don't imagine I irritate him either or he would make it obvious. I'm actually starting to get motivated and really loving my job more than ever. Our time at Uzman gave me plenty of time to rest and think about things. As long as I'm out here living the dream I've always had, I might as well be enjoying it a little bit. They told us that our mail is now being brought in by truck instead of flown in, that's why it's taking so long to get to us now. I wonder how much longer it's going to take, hopefully though it won't be too much longer. I'm still waiting to hear from those couple people I haven't heard from yet. I got a feeling I will hear from them soon, it will be nice to hear from them and be reassured they still care, it's been way too long. I've really learned a lot here in the last couple months. I've got to see being here who my true friends and family are, the people who matter and the ones who don't at all. I'm getting pretty excited for the ball when we get home. I'll probably end up spending way more money than I should but fuck it, we don't get to celebrate the Marine Corps birthday and coming home from Afghanistan every day in Vegas.

Mitchell Holmes and Corey Gibbs

June 5, 2011

Well we're right back to getting fucked over at Gumbatty, pissed off, and ready to go back to Uzman. We lost six guys today to 3rd platoon because they suck and had a bunch of guys sleeping on post, making them unreliable to stand post. I'm having fun though still and trying not to let it get to me too much. We got mail today and I finally got mail from the people I've been waiting to hear from for a long time.

June 6, 2011

I stood some post today, a couple times actually but it wasn't too bad, I got an unusual ten hours off in between and had no patrols today. Sergeant Amos from 1st platoon hit an IED today in the brown zone. The guys and I took a picture with the cigars that my Uncle Gary Hadlock sent, his one request was that we get a picture for him, we also took some moto boot pics today.

Back: William Baltes Front: Joseph Lechnar and
Mitchell Holmes with cigars from Mitchell's uncle,
picture taken by request from Gary Hadlock.

June 11, 2011

It's a cluster fuck here. We searched for
communications gear all day that WE didn't lose, then
in the end it turned out that it didn't even exist. People
are constantly fucking up, doing shit that gets us all in
trouble. We got word that we may be pushing south to
take over 2/8 AO in mid-July. It's more kinetic there
and the higher ups think the AUP have this area under
control, ha-ha. All the bullshit de motivates me but
I keep pushing on reminding myself that it will end
eventually. We're all ready to go home and have some
freedom, another thing we always took for granted. 1st
platoon has been in contact today for a good part of the
day, the most we've seen since we been here. Every
day I've been asking myself what the fuck we are here
for. What are we even really fighting for? Most of The

people here don't want us here and don't give a shit what we do for them or how many of us die here. Unless Marines plan to always occupy this country and protect them, we are wasting our time, the second we pull out, the ANA/AUP will strip off their uniforms, drop their weapons and run, they can't do it alone and I don't feel like they really want to. I'm ready to go home but at the same time, all the bullshit aside, I'm having fun and have been considering extending to stay in country an extra five months with the unit that will be relieving us. That way I could help them since I know the area and a lot of the people here. Maybe it would prevent them taking as many casualties. Everyone sure has it figured out what they plan to do when we get home and who they plan to do it with.

June 13, 2011

Lance Corporal Sean M. N. O'Connor from 3rd platoon was killed today by an RPG that struck his vehicle at their picket. He was a friend of mine but even closer friend of Gibbs. They knew each other from their last unit. When I think of Sean the same mental picture always pops up, of him smoking a big fat cigar almost every time I went outside to smoke on the weekends when I stayed in the barracks. That's the memory I'm going to try to keep of him. I always try to remember people by the good memories we had, I hate the last memory I have of a few people who are no longer alive. Bravo Company took nine casualties today. There's been lots of firefights lately. If guys keep getting in trouble it's going to make this deployment just creep by and keep getting worse. I'm ready to go home but at the same time wouldn't mind staying after all of our platoon has left, but with my luck the next unit would be horrible and make it miserable. All the guys already have it planned out in detail what they intend to do when they get home and who to do it with. I bet nine out of ten don't do anything even remotely close to their plans, myself included. It seems to always go that way.

June 15, 2011

We patrolled the green zone in search of IEDs today but didn't find any, we had to cross waist deep canals full of shitty dirty water. Things have really picked up in the Sangin valley, Bravo Company took six casualties yesterday, and they are getting hit harder up north than we are but the whole valley has been getting more action this month. The Taliban are massing up in the tree lines, setting IEDs with multiple secondary IEDs placed around it intended to get the guy who goes in to help his buddy, then cause a domino effect because they know we will go to help our buddies, etc. The platoon still pretty well hates each other. There's a feud between 1st and 2nd squad because they know they are fucking us over but just don't care. We will see how they like it when the balls in our court and we can return the favor. No they probably won't because we know who we are and help each other any chance we get, probably will for them too even though they are dicks and won't do shit for us. When 3rd squad gets here I'm sure they will take 1st squads place and it will be us against them for the same reasons. Some people and things never change. With all the casualties we've been taking lately we have been starting to wonder if we're going to make it home or not. We all joined the Marine Corps and came to Afghanistan knowing the risks but it's still weird to think about the possibilities of what could happen to us. We got a satellite phone for a week so I called and talked to my mom for a few minutes to let her know things are fine, I'm sure it helps her to talk to me, even if it is only for a few minutes. I don't call home very often partially because I don't want to sit and wait in line for the phone and partially to allow the family guys more time to talk to their wife and kids. It sounds like it's going to be intense if we push south, we still haven't heard any more about that yet though.

June 17, 2011

Unfortunately 3rd squad is here with us now and it's like fighting a whole different battle. 2nd squad pulls our weight plus some and 3rd gets to skate and just do enough to get by, it's noticed by everyone but changed by no one. Today I stood post for seven hours and when I got off we patrolled to the brown zone. I carried the ladder and provided over watch. While propped up on over watch I got to see some pretty good sized marijuana plants inside some of the compounds, there's a lot of them here.

June 19, 2011

Today is Father's day. The first father's day in my life that I'm not spending the day with my Dad as far back as I can remember, but I'm sure he's proud that I'm here. And I'm sure that my sisters will take him to dinner or something. Though I don't make very many calls home, I'm going to try harder to today so I can call him. We patrolled locally today but it seemed like such a long patrol after coming straight off the picket. Then went on post afterwards but now have a few hours off to rest before its post time again.

June 22, 2011

We now have to wear ballistic underwear that are supposed to save part of your legs if you get blown up. Hopefully we don't get to test them out even though I'm curious how well they work The PB took contact last night and returned fire. We also took contact while we were at the picket today. Four terrorists we're detained today after trying to place an IED near PB Wishtan. 2nd squad is waiting impatiently for our turn again to go to Uzman, hoping we get a couple more weeks there before the whole platoon moves over there to get a break from the bullshit. EOD came today and blew an IED that the Iskey found just on the other end of the bridge off of canal road. The Iskey are volunteer police who have their own little stations outside of our PB and some scattered, they aren't trusted enough yet to allow them to live inside with us, they have to put in a certain amount of time as Iskey before they can become AUP.

June 23, 2011

Some Major General stopped by today to check on the way we're doing things. We went to sleep when we found out he was coming and never ended up seeing him. Then we went on a five hour patrol to star wars and handed out old navy slippers and sunglasses that my

Mom has been sending me to hand out to the kids. They loved them, this is another form of trying to use counter insurgency to defeat our enemy. Winning the hearts and minds of the people and getting them to support our efforts. I had the thought too soon when I thought I had made it through the green zone for a whole patrol without getting wet and had to cross a god damn canal that was just within sight of the PB on our way back.

June 24, 2011

The tiger team arrived today, they are a team of mercenaries from different countries led by a British Marine named Nik Wilson. They seem to be well trained, motivated, alert, respectful, and blood thirsty, even their interpreter told me he does not know why but that he likes to shoot people. They are patrolling with us tomorrow so we will see if they are as hard as they appear to be.

June 25, 2011

We took the tiger team along on our patrol today. They wear a full combat load and are pretty locked on. They are as good as us if not better, it's definitely clear they have years of training and experience. When the platoon moves to Uzman one squad will be staying behind to work with them, I'm hoping it's us that stays. They are much easier to work with than the AUP, they actually act like they want to be here and are open to suggestions. And it would be nice to be here with just our squad. I turn twenty in ten days. I feel so young to be here, I can't even legally drink a beer in the

U.S. but I can be here risking my life for our country, something seems wrong with that system. It seems like just yesterday I was in high school with only a couple things on my mind. I feel pretty accomplished for only being twenty and having achieved what I have this far, following through with my goals in life.

June 26, 2011

We took the tiger team out with us again today. They seem to be pretty legit, there's a noticeable difference between them and the guys walking around in blue uniforms smoking hash being stupid that claim to be Afghan police.

June 28, 2011

I stood post for six hours then had some time off and was able to go talk with Nik Wilson for a while, the advisor of the Tiger Team. Then I went and talked to the guys in the Tiger Team and they were willing to trade stuff and they invited me to dinner and chai with them. He says they are anxious and looking for contact, he said the team is used to it being more kinetic and that if they can't find more contact around here soon they will have to keep moving to different patrol bases in different areas. I'm going to dinner with them tomorrow night.

June 29, 2011

We took the Tiger Team to the green zone today on a planned three hour patrol that turned into a seven hour patrol. They picked up some i com chatter talking about an RPG team that was set up on us waiting to hit us. As soon as they had the location of it, they attempted maneuvering on them but weren't quick enough to catch up with them. I couldn't believe the way they took off across open ground without sweeping for IEDs. We leave Friday to do our rotation at Uzman, I'm thankful that we get to go again before the whole platoon crams in there and we're all stuck together. I been handing out a lot of shoes and sunglasses to the local kids and it always makes them smile, get all excited then most of them thank me and call me their friend. It's amazing how happy shoes and sunglasses can make these kids. 1st platoon took three casualties today from a grenade but I haven't heard any details about what happened or who got hit yet.

June 30, 2011

Today was a shitty and life changing day for everyone in 2nd platoon. 3rd squad was patrolling right next to the picket inside a compound when Lance Corporal Childers stepped on an IED losing a leg, then shortly after Sergeant Chad D. Frokjer from Maplewood, Minnesota hit one too as he was calling in a 9 line to medevac Childers and unfortunately he didn't make it. I'm not going to go into detail because I don't want today's events and images to be stuck in anyone else's head for the rest of their life the way they will be in mine. Everyone is extremely affected by todays tragedy, of all people why him? A great, fair, knowledgeable leader and friend of everyone. He has a wife and unborn baby at home who will never get to meet his dad. I fucking hate this place and these people, you can't tell me that none of the people that live nearby there didn't know that compound was full of IEDs. Were full of anger and want revenge. We weren't the only unlucky ones today, the battalion took a lot of casualties today. It's been a horrible month for 1/5.

Sergeant Chad D. Frokjer at Mojave Viper training 2011.

July 1, 2011

We're at Uzman now for two weeks. Sergeant Elizondo made me one of the COGs while we are here, I'm glad he gave me the chance to prove myself as a leader and see what I got. I'm on eight hours on then eight hours off while we are here, same as the watch officer. The guys standing post are six hours on six hours off. It would be nice to have a couple more guys to be able to give them more time off at once but it's not going to happen.

July 2, 2011

The Sergeant Major stopped by today to tell us about leave and give us updates on the Battalions casualties. It's hard to think about leave knowing that we're not all going home together…It's pretty slow paced here since there's no one here to fuck with us. Sergeant Elizondo is stern but fair as long as we're doing what we're supposed to the way we trained to do it and not half assing everything. 1st squad found some IEDs today.

July 4, 2011

I celebrated this 4th of July roving posts, giving the guys on post breaks. Then just sleeping afterwards. Marines at Nolay fired some pyro off as fireworks and shortly after the whole valley lit up the sky with whatever they had on post with them. I doubt any of it was authorized but nothing was said about it to us, it brought some excitement into the day and changed things up from the normal day. If someone got in trouble for it, at least it's not any of us. Still in shock that Sergeant Frokjer is dead, it just doesn't seem like it can be real.

July 5, 2011

Today is my birthday, I'm spending it roving post and sleeping. It's just another day. I made it to twenty years old somehow. It would be nice to get some mail today though that would make the day a little bit better. 3/2 took small arms fire, an RPG and IDF today but no casualties. Lately it's been rare to go a day without someone getting wounded or killed. We been hearing that they are sending combat replacements but we sure haven't seen any yet, I'm not going to hold my breath on it. We did get some mail, it just got here, and the pillows came today that I asked my Mom to send us.

July 7, 2011

1st squad found an IED by the tower this morning, they are thinking someone may be sneaking in there close to the tower at night planting them. I been cooking everyday as COG, not sure how long it will last though me being COG because Gibbs got promoted to Corporal today. Which brings another issue I have with the way things work around here, that him and I are expected not to be friends anymore and for me to call him by rank because he picked up, its bullshit when we we're friends before and everything was just fine. We will probably play their games when they are around but when it's just us everything will be the same as it has been the whole time leading up till now.

July 8, 2011

The AUP brought back a detainee today that they claim is Taliban, we're not very clear on what their reasons are for accusing him or thinking that so we're sending him to FOB Jackson for them to investigate and decide for themselves if they think he is. The way he looks at us and his attitude make me think he's Taliban as fuck.

July 10, 2011

The tower had a grenade thrown at it in the middle of the night last night but no casualties, we been wondering when something would happen out there, it's so vulnerable when it's dark and they can simply watch and see there's only four of us out there at a time and only two up top on the platform at a time. We went and did a five man VCP outside Uzman today but didn't find anything out of the ordinary. We're all going to Gumbatty tomorrow for Sergeant Frokjer's memorial. It's going to be hard, being so soon after his death and doing the memorial so close to where he was killed. On Friday we move back there for a month, we're not really excited about it but there is a gym there now and one less post that has to be manned so maybe it won't be too painful.

July 12, 2011

Sergeant Frokjer's memorial yesterday was hard for everyone and very emotional for all of us but we can't drop our pack yet, we have to keep pushing, and that's what he would expect us to do.

July 14, 2011

Some General went around and visited the PBs today and decided that there needs to be two Marines on each post from 1900 to 0400 every night. Like that's possible when we're already hurting for extra guys. Gumbatty got rid of a post to help with it but also lost three guys that had to go to Uzman. What a god damn mess of shit. We're barely able to operate as it is and struggling to get one patrol a day out even with a smaller patrolling element. Us including our leadership thought the effort we have been giving was quite impressive but I guess not. We head back over to Gumbatty tomorrow.

July 16, 2011

We got to Gumbatty last night after being operation minimized for a day, then went on post. We're still operation minimized so when we got off post they sent us to do a VCP until we finally bitched enough about being the only ones that don't ever get a break that we got relieved for the day. I hate bitching so much but sometimes we just have to in order to stand up for ourselves and not get screwed.

July 18, 2011

We went and patrolled in the brown zone today and found a compound to do an over nighter in tonight then we will wake up and run two short patrols tomorrow. The PX truck is supposed to come tomorrow then we are going to the tower for two days, which is fine with me, I'll get to see my little friend Putagay that I have become pretty close to, that I consider my friend, who yells my name and comes running every time he sees me leave the wire then walks beside me till he gets side tracked by something else and takes off with his little buddies. Sometimes we walks beside me for hours.

Mitchell Holmes

July 19, 2011

We did our over nighter last night in the desired compound we had chosen throughout the day. It was quiet all night and the slab of concrete was almost as comfortable as a tempur pedic mattress. Not, it was horrible, I think we we're up most of the night smoking cigarettes. We went straight to patrolling the green zone from there and took a detainee out of compound 46. It seems to be more eventful inside Gumbatty than outside the wire at times.

July 21, 2011

I'm back at the tower for two days, not a whole lot happening out here today. The PX truck came today but we couldn't use the phone or internet because we're in river city from a casualty that occurred yesterday. 1/6 CO stopped by today to check out the PB and what we got going on. 1/6 is relieving 2/8 and extending their battlespace taking over Gumbatty so the whole platoon can move to Uzman. So all three squads will be back together and taking turns running patrols in the brown zone, sometimes running two patrols at the same time, it helps sometimes to have multiple patrols out at once.

July 23, 2011

1/6 is here now, we're doing the rip with them trying to prepare them for this area but they are Marjah Vets and just keep saying they got it, that it's not their first rodeo when we try to help them and tell them things are different here than Marjah. Whatever it's their funeral not ours, we can't make them listen and can't help them if they won't listen. Once we're done with them we can move over to Uzman. We patrolled yesterday then stayed out for an over nighter and patrolled back this morning. We went on QRF to the clinic down behind the bizarre trying to catch up with an insurgent who had been shot up north and fled south wounded. We ended up being four minutes late from when he was there trying to get aid. They snatched him up at the Gemille checkpoint.

July 25, 2011

2nd squad became a Mobile section and started moving the platoons stuff to Uzman. From what I can tell 1/6 is a relaxed and complacent unit. They been building seats in the posts, taking their gear off on post, stuff we wouldn't even think about doing. I predict them getting fucked up in the near future when the

Taliban notices that these guys don't pay any attention and are vulnerable. Even when we can't see them, they are always watching, trying to learn our patterns and find our weaknesses. But if they won't listen to us trying to help them, then it's their problem, we're out of here any day now whether they listen to us or not.

From left to right, William Baltes, Juan Rico, Mitchell Holmes and Joseph Lechnar playing Monopoly.

July 26, 2011

Baltes and I got to go to Nolay for the day to get the mine roller worked on, we were able to go use the internet for quite a while since there were no lines and the mine roller took most of the day to be fixed so we hungout at Nolay for the day. When we got back we had a big mound of mail waiting for us too. It was one of the best letter mail drops since we've been here. I finally got one from Sara, one of my best friends who I've remained friends with over the years no matter how far apart we are or how little we talk at times. Between her and my family it's motivated me to go home and I'm going to see if Sara wants to go to the Marine Corps Ball with me in November.

July 27, 2011

I didn't really do much of anything today. We just loaded a conex box then patrolled to Uzman to unload it then patrolled back to Gumbatty. When we got back we played monopoly the rest of the day and worked out a little bit. I could definitely go for more of these kind of days to relax and have some time to ourselves.

July 31, 2011

We've been patrolling a little bit but mostly just working on moving stuff to Uzman every day. 1st squad moved over there today, were moving on the second. Hopefully we will be as successful with our new AO as we have been with this one. Only two months left and hopefully we will all be going home together.

August 2, 2011

We got to Uzman for good yesterday, I stood a four hour post on the haunted post. We really think it's haunted because a Marine turned around killed an AUP for saying Taliban good, Marine no good while pointing his rifle at him. It always feels like someone is standing behind you when you're on that post, so I stand sideways so I can see behind me and outside. That post makes time drag by. Then we worked on our new gym until we went on patrol and explored our new AO. Found some firing points to blow up, made friends with some of the new areas kids, they don't even come close to being as badass as Putagay and the tower kids though. We Spent some time marking building numbers to make it easier in the future to recognize them, then went back and worked out. Things have been going pretty smoothly, smooth enough that it seems like something must be wrong. But hopefully it stays like this.

August 4, 2011

I saw a camel in the wild today for the first time in my life. Even looking at them it didn't seem real and still doesn't. I'm still experiencing culture shock. Gumbattys tower took IDF today. It raises our pride and confidence knowing the Taliban didn't want much of us but saw those guys weakness in just a couple days and acted on it. The company kept two squads from each platoon outside the wire for twenty four hours, 1st and 3rd squad looked like they were pretty worn out when they got back from that all day excursion. I got to talk to Ross on the phone tonight, he seems to be doing good and sounds a lot older than last time I talked to him. I worry about how he feels with me being gone.

August 5, 2011

The tower got hit again today and they ran out of ammo, we had to rush ammo to them. More post, there's nothing really new here. I'm having one of those fuck everything days, I don't give a shit to pick up rank or stay in any longer than I have to, I'm just sick of this shit and want to go home and get out. Motivation is really low for a lot of us right now and struggling to keep waking up every day.

August 6, 2011

Gunny Pate who was with EOD was killed today when he hit an anti-tampering device on an IED he was trying to disarm. The anti-tampering device hadn't been seen in this area until now, it's horrible that it happen in the first place but it's even worse he was doing the rip to go home soon.

August 7, 2011

We went on a five hour patrol today and took a couple guys from the army with us. I stayed back from the over nighter and put up camo netting over our gym to keep us out of the sun when we want to lift during daylight hours without getting burnt or being miserably hot, then I worked out a little bit and cleaned our nasty rat infested room.

August 8, 2011

Two of the battalions' snipers we're killed today by enemy snipers in Bravo Company's AO. We went on a seven hour patrol, wasn't too bad other than the scorching heat. Talked to Staff Sergeant about things around here, the transition home, etc. It was probably the best conversation him and I have ever had. We've been going on some long patrols lately but still have lots of time to work out so the few of us that do workout are perfectly content.

August 9, 2011

Today we went on a seven hour patrol, blew a compound and pissed off the neighbor because it took down part of his compound wall too on accident. He was fine with it once we explained that it would be paid for to be fixed and it may work out in our favor having a friend in the area. It did make a good video too, hopefully my camera keeps working after the blast. Sergeant Elizondo said I may go home with the advanced party but he's not sure yet, I have mixed feelings about it but really don't care either way if I go home early or stay.

August 10, 2011

The squad went on a six hour patrol today and found a possible IED we're going back to check out tomorrow. When we got back, Staff Sergeant passed some word and important upcoming dates. I've been talking to him a little bit lately when I run into him at the gym. I heard from Brianna today, one of my only friends that's stayed in contact since I've been deployed, well actually since high school. She's one of those few friends I don't have to talk to all the time to consider us close and I'm sure she feels the same way. Even when we go long periods of time without talking it's always the same like we talk every day.

August 11, 2011

We went and checked out that possible IED with EOD but it turned out to be nothing. One more day of patrolling then it's our turn to go on the post rotation for a few days. It's good to get a break and change things up a little bit so we're not doing the same things over and over again getting burnt out and complacent.

August 12, 2011

We finished this rotation off strong with a long ten hour patrol today, did a lot of short VCPs, now we're done patrolling for a few days. Then we go onto a different rotation, working long hours but we are learning a lot and getting to know the local people, we can already see a big change in their attitude towards us and they seem to really like us. It's a huge improvement over our first patrol over this way. They welcome us into their compounds now but won't let the other squads inside.

August 14, 2011

2nd squad went on an over nighter last night then spent the day doing VCPs. We're moving to Wishtan soon after Uzman is demilitarized and the ANA take over the posts that will be left on the uphill end of the PB. They don't need and can't handle the whole patrol base the way it is now.

August 16, 2011

Corporal Amador led todays patrol, it went pretty good, and smooth. I think we have a unique and impressive squad, we all get along really good and kick ass at everything we do working together, even when it comes to changing up everyone's billet to experience other positions, and we still dominate.

August 17, 2011

I'm the acting team leader today, calling in position reports, etc. Mostly stuff I already know but haven't done a lot of and don't get a lot of practice at, so todays the day. Today's patrol went smooth and boosted my confidence and motivation a little bit. Sergeant Elizondo wants us ready to pick up our first boots when we get back in case they are there waiting for us to get back. I feel sorry for them if they are there, not knowing what to expect from their new leadership. Just kidding, I don't really feel bad. It happens to all of us and that's what makes us how we are.

August 18, 2011

Today we got lucky. Well At least the front half of the patrol did. Sergeant Elizondo was the sixth man and stepped on a switch, but it didn't detonate, I was right in front of him at the time. We pushed forward while the tail end of the squad pushed back. EOD came and blew it, they said it was a fifteen pound directional charge with a pressure plate and command wire as a secondary. It was facing east toward the direction we were going. We were told about it five days ago but the Intelligence we had said it was inside the compound not in the alley outside.

August 24, 2011

On today's patrol we took along the CO, 1st Sergeant and 3/7 CO. It wasn't too bad but long as fuck. And all of them being along makes us nervous even when we're not doing anything wrong. Black iron took a casualty today. No details yet but we aren't surprised after seeing the kind of undisciplined, unmotivated unit they are.

August 26, 2011

We went on two patrols today. The PX truck came today but the internet fucked up on us, pretty sure it was from Patton trying to download shit, slowing it all down then ruining it for everyone else, oh well though, we got on for a little bit and were able to stock up on protein and cigarettes. It's normally motivating but this time it sucked not even being able to say goodbye to everyone I was talking to when it quit working, now hoping they aren't worried since I just disappeared like that.

August 27, 2011

2nd squad patrolled up north today, then went on a short VCP, it wasn't too bad but we're all still tired. We're doing a company surge tomorrow, blowing a bunch of shit up and going to have lots of patrols out all at the same time hoping to flood the area and catch some fuckers slipping. It should be interesting, they are using a Bangalore and a bunch of wall charges to take down a real long and tall two foot thick mud wall to improve visibility from one of the posts at Wishtan.

August 28, 2011

A good friend of mine Lance Corporal Jeremy Thomas, another Oregonian lost his hand today on a rooftop that the owners of the compound claimed was clear beforehand. I feel bad for Thomas, but we got even with those toothless, worthless, assholes and Thomas is going to be fine.

August 29, 2011

We did a Mobile VCP today, and ran over one hundred people through the system. Today is the end of Ramadan so the city is going crazy and we're wondering what kind of havoc it could bring our direction so we're preparing for it.

William Baltes providing over watch of the bizarre near PB Gumbatty during a patrol.

August 30, 2011

We're patrolling today up to rhino. We had two guys jump off their motorcycle and take off running, they had a bag with two brand new fifteen pound jugs and brand new pressure plates to go along with them, so we took care of the two guys that were on the other bike acting suspicious like they were lookouts riding ahead to watch for us. That's two less out there for us to walk on and two less assholes that put them in the ground.

August 31, 2011

We made a trip down to Nolay today to get the vehicles worked on, got the mine roller fixed then were able to get on the internet until we went into river city and had to get off. When we got back to Uzman we went on an over nighter, I kind of like the over nighters, it gives me time to think, time away from the rest of the platoon and in a way reminds me of camping and makes me feel kind of at home.

September 2, 2011

We can now say we will be home next month. Right now they are saying we will leave Sangin the seventh of October, we're starting to count down the days like is December waiting for Christmas. We took Zebula and another AUP on patrol with us today. They aren't too bad and they do their best to do their job and learn from us.

September 3, 2011

The AUP patrolled with us again today, raided some mosques, Zebula doesn't give a shit what the locals think, and he's been kicking doors in, breaking windows and shit, doing whatever he wants. I think part of it may also be because he likes to see our reaction. After patrol then were doing an over nighter in vehicles for the surge.

September 4, 2011

Went on our miserable over nighter, then went and did a ten hour VCP with vehicles, the last guy before our equipment died popped 100% as a level two Kandahar prison escapee that was put in prison for emplacing IEDs, we can't kill him but we did make sure he will remember us, fuckin piece of shit, It's hard to sit there and look at them in the face, not be able to do anything other than turn them in to Nolay and not just lose it, so much rage thinking about what they have done to my friends and our country. Now going to go to sleep and preparing for tomorrows patrol.

September 6, 2011

The CO and 1st Sergeant went on patrol with us today. They didn't give any debrief points other than that it was a perfect patrol and they we're pleased with our performance. We're taking the BC with us tomorrow and only have one patrol planned so it shouldn't be too bad of a day if we can nail it tomorrow like we did today while he's along to see.

September 7, 2011

We took the BC along with us today, he said to keep up the good work and keep doing what we're doing and we'll make it out of here in one piece. He also said we make him proud and that we're the reason he's stayed in the Marine Corps. To lead Marines.

September 8, 2011

Alpha company did a company surge today. A suicide bomber with a VBIED attacked Comanche on the 611 resulting in one routine casualty and four civilian KIAs. 3rd squad found an IED in the process of being emplaced that appeared was being emplaced when the patrol came into the area. Then they found some grenades and IED making materials in a nearby compound so we will now be putting more time and pressure on that area to see what else we can find.

September 9, 2011

We patrolled to the south today, it's a pretty shady looking area. It's hard to explain it but some of these places and the people just put off a negative energy that makes us suspicious, kind of like when the music changed in the immersion trainer at Camp Pendleton right before an attack. We found some IED making materials, regardless of what the people think and say, the Taliban are very much still here and not backing off anytime soon, but neither are we and neither will the Marines that come in the future. If they haven't figured it out yet, Marines won't give up unless we're dead or it's a decision that's out of our control.

September 10, 2011

We got a spot report for a VBIED and four suicide bombers in our AO looking to celebrate tomorrow being the anniversary of 9/11 by hitting us with multiple complex attacks, we're hoping they show their pussy little faces so we can send them all to meet their 72 virgins. The reports we are getting are saying that a suicide bomber will initiate the attack, followed by small arms fire, then secondary bombers. It could turn into a fucked up day for us but only time will tell to see if there's any truth to any of it. We have had plenty of reports that have turned out to be nothing but we have to take everything serious and expect that it is going to happen and to expect the worst case scenario. We hope for the best but expect the worst. We got our shit wired tight and ready for anything those illiterate cowardly son of a bitches throw at us. We got less than a month and we are out of this shithole of a country.

September 12, 2011

Well there were no attacks yesterday, we spent seven hours on a mobile VCP without the proper and needed equipment to run people through the system to see if there are any idiots who think they can just walk through without getting caught. Then we got back to the PB and got ready and went on an over nighter to compound number twenty one. It was the same as usual but I've been starting to think that these are times I will look back on years down the road and miss in ways. I'm sure there's a lot about this deployment that I will look back on my whole life and miss in ways. In three weeks we will be leaving Sangin, probably will never come back, and in thirty eight days I will get a break from these assholes I been living with for six months. Love these guys to death but we've all spent way too much time together. I don't know what to look forward to the most about going home.

September 13, 2011

As soon as we got back from our over nighter we went right back out on another patrol. EOF was used by 1st squad today on a red Toyota corolla who ignored the signals and continued to drive towards their VCP. Rico fired and a round ricocheted off the driver's forehead and hit the passenger in the ass, they then stopped and the passenger got out yelling at the driver for not stopping. The passenger was a friend of the platoon and didn't want trouble, the driver said he didn't see us. We're moving to Wishtan soon, no one is very excited but it's what we have to do, we would all rather just be with 2nd platoon than up there with half the company. But most of all we are just ready to get out of here. Whatever it takes to be closer to our journey home.

September 15, 2011

1st squad found an IED in an alley that we haven't been down since one of our first patrols in April. Black iron had a double amputee occur today. Just outside the wire, within sight of their PB. Someone wasn't doing their job for that to happen.

September 16, 2011

PB Dash took two RPGs today, Lance Corporal Harris took shrapnel to the face, neck, and chest but other than some cosmetic damage will be fine. We got to see a picture of Thomas with the commandant getting his purple heart but he doesn't look like he's very happy about any of it, we all feel bad for him, Thomas is a friend of everyone, we all wish so badly that there was something we could do.

September 17, 2011

Patrolled to the south this morning, wasn't too bad, our patrols have gotten easier. Rico pulled out some boxing gloves so we been having boxing matches and beating the shit out of each other when we have spare time and to release the tension. We're making a trip to Nolay tonight to do our PDHA, one more check in the box to be able to go home.

September 19, 2011

We Went to Nolay and spent all day there, that was pretty motivating. We come up with more and more plans by the day of what we want to do when we get home but probably won't end up doing most of it. I bet we all kind of keep some distance for a while. Baltes about rolled the MRAP on the way up to Dash, he swears it slid off the road but I watched it drive off the road so that tells me he just wasn't paying attention and is trying to cover his tracks now and embarrassed that we saw him do it.

September 20, 2011

Only one patrol today, then 2nd squad went to Gumbatty to get ammo counts and covered for the guys at the tower so they could go to the PB and do counts. It was a fun but emotional day, got to see Putagay and the tower kids for the last time ever. They were pretty excited to see us after not seeing us for a while. I'm actually going to miss Putagay, in fact I already do and we haven't even left yet, just knowing I'll never get to see the kid again sucks. Patrols have continued to keep getting easier. Not wanting to take any chances this close to getting out of here.

September 21, 2011

A Marine in Afghanistan killed himself while on post. A place where many things run through your head. I'll be the first to admit I've thought of plenty of crazy stuff while on post but I've never been in that kind of mental state. I've heard people say my whole life that suicide is selfish and cowardly but I strongly believe that we who have never been in the situation cannot fully understand or judge people who commit suicide because we don't understand where they were at mentally.

September 23, 2011

Woke up today and heard that a mine roller on the 611 ran over a motorcycle and killed the woman on it and broke the man's leg who was riding with her. Kind of a shitty deal but understandable since they drive wherever they want and don't pay attention to where they are going and who they pull out in front of. Lance Corporal Aicher left today with the advanced party and should be home in less than a week. They picked him to go because he has kids, which I'm totally fine with. As for us, 3/7 should be arriving within the week then we will be flying out of Nolay on the 5th. Corporal Amador's son was born today. He's pretty excited and anxious to get home and meet him., I can't imagine how he must feel. We all have big plans and are more than ready to head home. The flight home is going to seem like forever. Our patrols are to the minimum, it seems like they have amounted to walking out the wire, sitting down for five hours, then walking back into the PB. No one is taking the chance of getting blown up when we're this close to going home. Sergeant Elizondo was selected for Staff Sergeant so he will be leaving us shortly after we return home, followed by others who are going to other units or have reached the end of their contracts and have decided to get out of the Marine Corps. Every day I ask myself new questions and not sure exactly what to do or how to find the answers for what I should do.

September 25, 2011

This morning we got back from a cold over nighter, it probably wasn't really that cold but with the heat the way it's been the last six months it sure felt like Oregon weather. The Engineers are here and started the process of demilitarizing PB Uzman. We Worked on that until our afternoon patrol, then went and sat in compounds eating pomegranates all afternoon. Patrol intentions haven't slowed down a bit and don't look like they are going to. 2nd squad is staying here to provide security for the engineers until the demil is complete, while the rest of the platoon is on their way to Wishtan to run patrols until we leave Sangin. It should take a few days to be completed.

September 28, 2011

The demil is in the process. Last night one wall was completely down so we had a rooftop post to be able to see all the way around us. It was weird sitting on post half the night being so exposed. It's pretty shady now with three walls down, 1st squad is coming tonight for support in case something was to happen. As ready as I am to leave I'm going to miss this place in a weird fucked up way, I'm already thinking about coming back. I'm sure my parents and family wouldn't approve but they are pretty supportive when it comes to doing what makes me happy. I almost feel depressed, maybe nervous about the transition home. I feel like I've become socially awkward being here and don't know how to talk to people anymore. I think it's going to be difficult adjusting to life again that doesn't consist of doing the same thing day after day, not bathing often, living like there is no tomorrow, eating out of bags, and being used to being around guys all day every day for seven months talking about anything we want to.

August 2, 2011

We're at Wishtan now, preparing everything to go home and starting to go over how things will happen when we get home, what's expected of us, and what the plans are as soon as we have been back awhile, decompressed, and are ready to do it all over again. We're not even home yet and they are already talking about the next one. I went on my last patrol today, as we were getting close to the end we spotted a possible IED and had to wait for two hours so EOD could come and check it and all they ended up doing was walked up to it and pulled it out of the ground without having to investigate it even. It's weird to think that I'm done patrolling and standing post but still won't be home for a couple weeks. I don't really know how to even explain how I feel about everything right now. I'm so happy and so thankful to be going home but at the same time I'm not ready to leave and feel guilty that I survived and that there's so many guys who didn't make it and don't get to return home to their families.

August 7, 2011

We're at Camp Leatherneck now for a little bit, the beginning of our decompression to reenter the real world. Gibbs and I have still been hitting the weights hard and non-stop talking about what to do when we get home. It's hard to get in on a computer with so many guys in the USO who are trying to use the few computers they have in there available. Time is creeping by slower than it has the last seven months. It's like waiting for opening day of deer or elk season or the night before leaving on a camping trip, it feels like it's never going to get here and the more things you do to try to pass time, the slower it goes.

August 19, 2011

We are back to Camp Pendleton now, it's like culture shock all over again, America is even more amazing than I had ever remembered it. I was welcomed home tonight by my family and Bryanna and Steve Kessler. I could tell that my parents were relieved that I'm home.

My Mom said the only time in seven months that she was okay was when we were on the phone. I can only imagine what it's been like on their end the last seven months, never knowing what was going on other than the few minutes they were on the phone with me or the letters they got that I had written weeks before they actually got them or worst of all, everything that they were hearing was happening to the battalion day after day and the guys close to us that didn't make it home.

December 8, 2015

As I finish typing I'm thinking about a lot of things in detail that I hadn't thought about for a long time. And I look back at how quickly my attitude went back and forth throughout the deployment. There's things I really miss about it but many things I don't either. Since we returned home there has been a lot of things happen that change my views and opinions on a lot of the stuff I talked about through this book. Reading through and typing reminded me of things that I had forgotten and some things I think about daily and only wish I could forget. Our deployment to Sangin had both positive and negative outcomes for all of us. I made lifelong friends who all stay in contact and check on each other, I accomplished the first part of my childhood dream and I was forced to grow up quickly. I also got an experience that I can always look back on when I start to think something is hard or undoable and tell myself I've done harder things. Only a couple of the guys I mentioned are still active duty, but all living and stay in contact with one another. As for me now, I have been married almost four years, have two beautiful little girls, Diamond who is 2 years old and Peyton who's a newborn. We have decided to settle down in Rainier, Oregon. I chose to follow my father's footsteps again and have went into the logging industry. Logging for R.D. Reeves Construction Inc., the company my Dad retired from a couple years back. I have a close and caring family that reminds me to live every day. Many troops have a rough time after coming home, if one said they didn't or still don't they are either lying or had a much different experience than us. For everyone who has taken the time to read this far, please remember that not all wounds are visible. Please support our troops now serving and veterans from all of our nation's wars.

Tim Cahill, Teresa Cahill, Mitchell Holmes,
and Sara Holmes at the Marine Corps Ball
in Las Vegas in November 2011.

Gone But Not Forgotten

LCPL JOE M. JACKSON 24-APR-2011
LCPL RONALD D. FREEMAN 28-APR-2011
LCPL NICHOLAS S. O'BRIEN 9-JUN-2011
LCPL JOSHUA B. MCDANIELS 12-JUN-2011
LCPL SEAN M. O'CONNOR 12-JUN-2011
LCPL JARED C. VERBEEK 21-JUN-2011
CPL GURPREET SINGH 22-JUN-2011
GYSGT RALPH E. PATE, JR 26-JUN-2011
LCPL JOHN F. FARIAS 28-JUN-2011
SGT CHAD D. FROKJER 30-JUN-2011
CPL KYLE R. SCHNEIDER 30-JUN-2011
LCPL NORBERTO MENDEZ-
HERNANDEZ 10-JUL-2011
LCPL ROBERT S. GRENIGER 12-JUL-2011
SGT DANIEL J. PATRON 6-AUG-2011
SGT ADAN GONZALES, JR. 7-AUG-2011
SGT JOSHUA J. ROBINSON 7-AUG-2011
CPL MICHAEL J. DUTCHER 15-SEP-2011

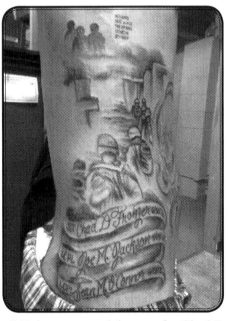

Mitchell Holmes memorial tattoo for Chad Frokjer, Joe Jackson, and Sean O'Connor. Artwork by Brandon Whitaker of Surreal Skin in Longview, Washington.

Printed in the United States
By Bookmasters